Stallion on a Frozen Lake

Stallion on a Frozen Lake

Love Songs of the Sixth Dalai Lama

TRANSLATED BY COLEMAN BARKS

Maypop Books
191 East Broad St., Suite 202
Athens, GA 30601
1-800-682-8637

Composed by Briarpatch Press, Davidson, North Carolina
Printed by Thomson-Shore, Inc., Dexter, Michigan

The Sixth Dalai Lama

(1683–1706, maybe 1746)

Rigdzin Tsangyang Gyatso. *Gyatso*, the lineage. *Rigdzin* means "treasure." *Tsangyang* came from a precognitive dream that a monk had about him. It means, "having a voice like God's." The sweetness of these songs in Tibetan has always been associated with his voice-melody. They are treasured throughout the Himalayan region, and up until the 1950's when street-singing was outlawed by the Chinese communists, they were heard in the markets of Lhasa. The reality they embody, of being drawn simultaneously by the clarity of meditation and by the delights of desire, and the ground they find that mixes those, is felt as the great gift of his art. The songs are modeled on anonymous folksongs sung in a lilting manner. They treat love problems in simple images and plain, intense speech. His street name, Dangwang Bangpo, means "one who has a good sensual appetite."

The early part of Tsangyang Gyatso's life was lived in secret confinement with his tutors, evidently to preserve the politically expedient illusion that the Fifth Dalai Lama was still alive, and on retreat. In 1697 at the age of 14, his public life began. He was enthroned with great ceremony as the Sixth Dalai Lama. But he turned out to be a unique sort of holy man. He seems to have formally "given back" the monastic vows he took. He lived in the Potala (the monastery palace), but dressed as a layman. He wore rings and blue silk, instead of the red and yellow of the monks. He kept his hair long, and on most days was to be found out in the archery field with his friends. He had a free-roving spirit, and he loved to take short journeys "according to his will." He is best remembered now, of course, for his nights, which he spent with many different partners, aristocratic women from Lhasa and peasant girls from Shol, the village at the foot of the Potala. His love-life and the poems he wrote from within it are a cultural treasure. It was an honor to have the Sixth Dalai Lama visit one's daughter for a night. Houses were painted yellow as a sign that the privilege had occurred, and it is said that a good percentage of the houses were yellow, as opposed to the traditional white.

There are many different tones in his love songs—urgency, caution, tenderness, wry humor, confusion, pleading—the variety found in all love poetry. We get a sense of a growing, energetic human being, amused by his predicament, being so young and carrying such light. There's an interesting contemporary account of a traveler (Lelung) who came to a house late where the Sixth Dalai Lama and his retinue were. All the attendants were drunk and behaving stupidly, but Tsangyang was "completely clear, writing songs, and singing them without flaw, not in the least affected by the alcohol." And the man who caused the early downfall of the Sixth reminisced remorsefully, "He had wonderful charm, and he was tremendously bold. He knew he was not destined to live beyond the age of twenty-five." The word "bold" is used here in the sense of someone who acts with courageous resolve on the difficult path toward enlightenment. Tsangyang Gyatso was an honest, and open, rebel, who would no doubt laugh at any attempt to characterize his behavior. He was not chaste. He was not profligate. He had a fine sensitivity and a taste for the company of any and all elements of the human community.

I hear Shakespeare, Sappho, Byron, Keats, Wyatt, Elvis and Van Morrison in these poems, Chaucer, Ovid, Emily Dickinson, and the troubadors. He is not simple! And he's still very controversial: A tantric master, a libertine, or some as yet unnameable mixture? In 1706, he was publically declared by one governing element *not* to be the incarnation of the Great Fifth, deposed, and led off toward China. Monks loyal to him, though, freed him and took him to the summer palace. After a short siege he surrendered himself to avoid more fighting, and the journey toward China resumed. According to Chinese records, on November 14, 1706, he died and was cremated near Lake Kokonor. But the story doesn't end there.

Fifty years later in Mongolia a book appeared which claimed to be his secret biography, saying that he didn't die in 1706 but magically escaped, assumed a disguise, lived in a hermit's cave, and then began a new life as a wandering pilgrim, traveling to Nepal, India, throughout Tibet and China, and living finally as an abbot of a Mongolian monastery. The secret biography is evidently very plausible, and accepted as genuine by the current Tibetan community in exile. After his disappearance in 1706 the Chinese tried to replace him with their own candidate for "the true Sixth," but the stand-in was never accepted by the Tibetan people. The lineage continued out of Lithang, as Tsangyang Gyatso had predicted it would in a poem sent secretly back from the exile journey to an unidentified woman.

The brother of the current Dalai Lama tells the story of how an old man came to Tsangyang's tent opening there as he was camped by Lake Kokonor in 1706. "Who are you?" asked the young Dalai Lama.

The old man replied, "Sengge," which means "lion." The name of the nearby lake meant "joy." "The lion's happiness. A sign that I should leave my people here, so they can be happy." And saying this, he left, never reclaiming his place as the Sixth Incarnation, though several times he is said to have appeared in Tibet in various disguises. At the following year's New Year festival in Lhasa, for example, the ruling regent saw a beggar and bowed as he would only bow to the Dalai Lama. People noticed and cried out, but the beggar disappeared. The same thing happened with the state oracle at Nechung. He suddenly turned and paid homage to a particular man in the crowd, who immediately vanished. The legend continues, how he traveled as a mendicant to the shrines of India, and also worked as a shepherd for a wealthy Mongolian lady. One day she complained that a wolf was killing the sheep. Armed with just a small knife, he went into the hills and brought the animal back alive, "Here is the wolf. Punish him however you wish." Tsangyang's legend-laced wandering is what he leaves us, along with the short poems, which are themselves close to the texture of his moving. Perhaps the truth he embodies is that, more than scriptures and religious disciplines, life-lived is the great teacher. We have the shape of a foundation, but his temple remains a mystery.

Michael Tatz suspects that Tsangyang's actual diary of the early years exists, or a copy, and that the diary is the ultimate source of the songs. If that precious document does exist, it could clarify some of the problems in the poems. Perhaps it will appear. The cloak of mystery still very much surrounds the Sixth. The Thirteenth Dalai Lama in conversation with Charles Bell said, "Tsangyang Gyatso used to have his body in several places at once, in Lhasa, in Kongpo, and elsewhere. He has one tomb in Alashan in Mongolia and another in Drepang in Tibet. Showing several bodies at the same time is disallowed now because it causes confusion in the work."

Whatever the truth, the multiple energies that compose the Sixth Dalai Lama are powerfully elusive. They confuse normal concepts of identity, and they make his poetry very alive to the touch.

Sources

Michael Aris, *Hidden Treasures and Secret Lives, A Study of Pemalingpa (1450–1521) and the Sixth Dalai Lama (1683–1706),* Motil Banarsidass (Delhi, 1988), pp. 107–226.

Songs of the Sixth Dalai Lama, translated by K. Dhondup, Library of Tibetan Works (Dharmsala, 1981).

Wings of the White Crane, Poems of Tshangs dbyangs rgya mtsho (1683-1706), translated by G.W. Houston, Motilal Banarsidass (Delhi, 1982).

Michael Tatz, "Songs of the Sixth Dalai Lama," *The Tibet Journal,* VI, no. 4 (1981), pp. 13–31.

Thubten Jigme Norbu and Colin Turnbull, *Tibet,* Simon & Schuster (New York, 1968), "A Riddle of Love," pp. 279–294.

This young man slyly manages
to steal a supply of truth.

From under the cap he wears out
a pigtail swings down the back.

Even the stars can be measured,
their arrangements and influences.

Her body can be lovingly touched,
but not her deep longings.

Those cannot be understood
by science.

Lassoes can catch the wild horses
that flee over the hills.

But nothing, not even incantations,
can hold a wild beloved

who has stopped loving
her lover.

The carved horse on the ferryboat
turns toward me, feeling nothing.

My lover going away on the same boat
doesn't look back. She feels
less than nothing.

I have planted prayerflags
to protect my Beloved.

You wanderer through the forest,
Ajo Shelngo, don't kick them down!

The ink of lovesongs
washes off in the rain,
but the love itself,

that which cannot be
written down, stays
inside *here*.

The pressed wax that legalizes documents
cannot testify in court for you.

It's better to seal your love
with the honesty of clear discernment.

The branch of blossoming hollyhocks
goes as an offering to the altar.

"Please," begs the turquoise bee,
the young one, "take me with you!"

If the one I love gives up everything
to study the teachings,
I'll take the holy path too.

I'll live in a secluded retreat
and forget how young I am.

I listen intently
to what my teacher says,
but beneath that concentration

my loving slips
out of the room
to be with you.

In meditation, the face of my teacher
does not come to me very clearly,

but your face does, smiling one way,
then smiling another.

If I could meditate as deeply
on the sacred texts as I do

on you, I would clearly be
enlightened in this lifetime!

Your stallion trots on the slippery ice,
over deep-frozen and nearly-frozen water.

When you move toward the beauty of a new lover,
be careful that your secret legs
don't scatter and fall!

In Lhasa, the crowds thicken.
In Chungyal, people are friendly,
and charmingly placed.

The lover I'm longing for now
lives in the Chungyal valley.

The old dog at the gate
has a more subtle soul
than most human beings.

Please don't tell them
how I left at dusk
and came back in at dawn!

It was snowing at nightfall
when I went out to look for my lover.

Now the secret of where my feet went
is openly visible to everyone.

Lover waiting in my bed
to give me your soft, sweet body,
do you mean well?

What will you take off me,
besides my clothes?

White crane!
Give me your long wings.
I won't fly far.

I'll come back.
From Lithang.

(A prediction of where the next incarnation of the Dalai Lama would be born.)

A peacock from Bengal,
a parrot from eastern Tibet,

they come together at Lhasa
in sacred companionship.

The willow loves the sparrow.
The sparrow lives lovingly
inside the willow.

What can the grey hawk do
to lure the sparrow out?

Devil thorns at my back,
dangerously fierce.

Apples in front of me,
deliciously ripe.

I'm wary of thorns,
so I have decided,
once and for all,

to pick and eat
the apples.

The swan wants to stay longer,
and longer, with the lake it loves.

But when ice covers the surface,
the swan flies, with no regrets.

Late frost on the blossoms,
a cold wind. They must have come

to keep the bees from climbing
into the flowers.

What appears in Spring
fades in the Fall.

The blue-green bees
don't mourn that destiny.

My lover and I will not always be together,
but we don't cry about it.

The moon tonight is full,
but where is the peaceful rabbit

who usually appears
inside the circle?

The battering wings of this eagle!
The wind and the difficult rocks.

Those who oppose me
never let up.

My childhood friend,
you must be kin
to wolves!

After so many nights together,
you still want to run loose
through the hills.

At night, I'm so in love
I can't sleep, and each day

fills with the fatigue
of not having you again.

Wanting this landlord’s daughter
is wanting the topmost
peach.

Your body smells so sweet,
my lover on the road.

A white turquoise stone,
not worth much, found,
then thrown.

If I could live with the one
I love, I would know the secret

that the ocean keeps
in its deepest bed.

Yesterday's new-green shoots
are straw now.

Think of your young body
bent and stiff,

like a dried-out
bamboo bow.

The full moon lifts
over the hill edge.

Inside, I see
you smiling.

Back when I was lucky,
I could hoist a prayerflag,

and some well-bred young woman
would invite me home.

She shone her whole smiling face
at the crowd in the tavern.

Then, from the delicate corners
of her eyes, she spoke
love-secrets to me.

Intrigued, and wanting her,
I asked if she wanted me.

"Only death could prevent us,"
she answered. "In this life,
nothing will keep us apart."

Doing what my darling wants
will weaken my surrender
to the sacred teachings.

On the other hand, if I retreat
to a mountain hermitage, it would crush
her tenderness toward me.

I'm young, so
with a slight smile
you have me.

But what I want
is a word from the stream
of your being.

I was a solitary hunter.
I caught the sky-girl, Yitrog Lhano,

but Norzang Gyalu, a lord
of men, took her from me.

When I had the priceless jewel,
I didn't consider its value.

Now that no one has it,
the knowledge of what that was
breaks over me like the first sad morning.

One who loved me
has been given in marriage to another.

My body grows thin and sick
with what now cannot be.

I often see my lost lover in dreams.
I will ask a shaman to search in there
and bring her back to me.

If my lover lives forever,
if wine never stops pouring,

if this tavern keeps standing,
sheltering us, that's enough!

Is this girl human,
or did she come from a stem
on the branch of a peach tree?

Her love opens and withers and falls
just as quickly as those flowers.

The moon goes away, marking
the end of a month. Gone a few days,

like my lover and I. Then,
it comes up new.

Rirab Lhunpo, golden Sumeru, mountain
at the center of the universe,
stay solid and still,

so the moon and the sun
can revolve without
wandering off.

On the third day, the moon appears
like my lover in white silk.

By the fifteenth day, our meeting
has grown brighter and more direct.

Oracle of the Tenth Stage,
Dorje Choskyang, if you have power,
destroy those who hate the natural law.

The bird has come that brings wetness
from Tawang, where I was born,
to the fields here.

I have met my deep lover.
Now I can rest.

Animals of all kinds can be tamed
with bits of meat and bread.

But this tavern tigress, when you think
she's satisfied, she rises
to snarl again.

My lover and I, we meet in complete
privacy, in the southern valley forest.

Then I hear some parrot in the market
jabbering our secrets.

We’ve had our short walk together,
this joy. Let’s hope we meet early
in the next life, as young lovers.

The glowing pink clouds
conceal a cold front
and a hailstorm.

Someone who is halfway a monk
hides and destroys the wisdom.

While I live in the monastery palace,
I am Rigdzin Tsangyang Gyatso,
honored in the lineage.

When I roam the streets in Lhasa,
and down the valley to Shol,

I am the wildman, Dangzang Wangpo,
who has many lovers.

The fierce Lord of Death, Yama,
will give me what I have coming.

Here, while alive, I haven't expected,
or gotten, any justice.

She puts on her hat and leaves,
slinging her hair back,
waving goodbye.

“I’m sad that you’re going,”
I say. “Don’t feel sad, my love,”
she said, “Every going-away
brings a coming-together!”

The arrow hit the target, cut through,
and stuck in the ground on the other side.

Now that I have met my Beloved, my loving
follows her, all by itself.

People are talking about me.
I’m sorry for what I’ve done.

I took three baby steps
and found myself drunk
in my lover’s arms.

Parrot, would you quit talking,
please? *Close your mouth!*

The thrush in the willow
has promised me a song.

Pure snow-water from the holy mountain.
Dew off the rare Naga Vajra grass.

These essences make a nectar
which is fermented by one
who has incarnated as a maiden.

Her cup's contents can protect you
from rebirth in a lower form,

if it is tasted in the state
of awareness it deserves.

I have never slept
without a lover.

Nor have I ever let
one drop of sperm come.

I know her body's softness,
but not her love.

I draw figures in sand
to measure great distances
through the sky.